Social Media Chaos: What was The World like before Its Explosion and how is it shaping the minds of People Today

I0481400

By Stan Kennedy

Table of Contents

Introduction

You must have heard the term social media... I mean, who wouldn't? You probably got the link to this eBook from one. The world has really come a long way with social media as it is, and has been made a smaller place literally because of these new tools of communication. Someone once said that social media is word of mouth on steroids. As amusing as that statement is, it has a ton of truth in it. However, it seems a lot of internet users are getting overdosed on that "steroid" leading to desirable and undesirable outcomes that we will discuss in subsequent chapters. The main purpose of this eBook to look at social media as a concept; its inception and explosion; the good and the not-so-good impact it has had on our society and the world at large; the way out and forward with social media. Here is breakdown of what each chapter entails;

In the introductory chapter, we look at social media from a light perspective: what it is; what it benefits are; general overview of functions; how to get started; privacy considerations; and a few safety tips for using any of these platforms.

In chapter two, we look at what the world was like before the advent of social media; the modes of communication that preceded social media, and how they worked.

In chapter three, we look at several definitions of the term social media from different sources and what social media is and what it's not. We also get into why it was invented and how it became a global means of communication.

In chapter four, we have a look at how social media has impacted this generation, both old and young; its positive and negative impact, and the causes of these impacts.

In chapter five, we go on to look at how social media is and can be used to control the human mind (shocker alert!).

In chapter six, we take into consideration what we have gained since the evolution of social media and what we have lost as well. Chapter seven discusses the way out and forward with social media, while we draw our conclusions in that last and final chapter.

Right now, the question remains...

What is social media?

The term social networking is usually intertwined in the definition of social media as a concept. While social networking fundamentally entails the use of the internet to link users together, social media, as the term suggests, are the avenues through which it is done. However, social media platforms such as websites (and apps) are not really about meeting new users online, even though that tends to happen every other day. Rather, they are basically about linking up with family, friends, colleagues, and acquaintances that the user already familiar with.

So in general, social media is an internet-based platform for communication. They allow users to have conversations, distribute information and also create web content. There are several forms of social media, including blogs, micro-blogs, picture-sharing sites, wikis, social networking sites, instant messaging, video-sharing sites, podcasts, widgets, virtual worlds, and much more.

Amongst the top/most popular social media platforms are Facebook, Twitter, LinkedIn, Instagram, and YouTube. All these allow users to generate and distribute information in the form of texts, photos, videos and, organise events (both online and offline), and take part in online gaming.

The connections between users are not singular, but rather a network consisting of several connections. This online social network is useful for sending out information and typically keeping in touch with people you would often not have opportunity to relate with.

What are the benefits of using social media?

Around the globe the use of social media to create and spread information and link up with other users has almost become second nature. Personally, most social media platforms enable you to reach family and friends, acquire knowledge and skills, develop and further your own interests, and also regale yourself. As regards your career, you can utilize opportunities provided by social media to extend your knowledge and skills in any field and build your connection with other professionals in your, and any, industry. Social media can also serve as a means for you to converse with your clients, and promote your business. We'd get into more of the profound positive change that social media has brought to our world.

Getting started

It can be a very overwhelming experience for some to choose which social media platforms is the right one that fit their needs given that there are a myriad of them out there, with more springing up almost every day. This being the case it is important to get yourself acquainted with a few of these platforms, and wrap your head around which one of them meets your communication needs. However, bear in mind that not all social media will be compatible with your communication goals, and there also isn't a one-size-fits-all; usually a combination of 2 or 3 may better than just one. So then if you are contemplating signing up on a social media platform, you can inquire from a family member or perhaps a friend who is conversant with the website of your choice to give you a hand in setting you up and teach you how to use basic functions of the site. At first it might seem a tad complex when you get started but as soon as you get with the system you will find it a lot easier to navigate.

In addition, before you create a social media account for your business do well to study how other companies use the platform. Ask yourself: what type of information is allowed on the site? Which contents are trending on the site? And how often are posts made on the site by companies? Then, think carefully about how your business would fit in.

It's very important to be aware that just because you can be on a social media platform, doesn't really mean you should be. Spreading yourself thin across several social media could dampen the effectiveness of your communication. This will also prevent you from really getting the best of any of them. Instead, channel your energy and resources towards the social media sites that let you share content with the right audience.

Your profile page

Usually when you set up a social media account you may need to provide your active email address to validate your identity, and then your profile page will be created automatically. Subject to the platform you are using, a profile page would allow you post some information about yourself and your interests, this usually includes a photograph. Your "friends" or "fans" will be able to view your profile page and the information you upload. They may, depending on the privacy setting, be able to post comments or share information with you on your profile page. When setting up your profile, it's not mandatory to fill all the fields. Think critically about what details about yourself that you want others to know right before you upload it. Although most, if not all, social media platform allow you to edit any information about yourself you uploaded previously.

Privacy

As stated earlier, social media websites have a quite a number of privacy settings that you can tweak. This invariably means that you have control over who sees your profile page and any other information you may share. A few people really do not give a care about allowing their personal information to be available for anyone else to see online. However, it isn't advisable to publish information that may generally be considered too sensitive such as date of birth, home address, even full names, including those of others, be they family or friend. It is important to be aware that if the wrong parties gain access to your sensitive personal data such full name and date of birth, social security number, and other available information it is quite possible that you could fall prey to identity thieves. So, in the same way you would not give your phone number or bank details to just anyone who asked, you should restrict access to all personal details posted in your social media accounts.

A few people prefer only to allow those they have officially become friends with to view their profile page. It is of import to note that the preset option setting for most social media platforms (Facebook inclusive) is to keep your personal information open to all when you sign up at first. It is up to you, if you do not want your profile to be viewed by people who are not a "friend" or "follower," to check your profile options and tweak them accordingly.

Friends and "friends"

The main aim of signing up on social media is to keep in touch with your family, friends. Having "Friends" in social media context (especially Facebook), has a specific meaning. For instance, for you to communicate online with other users such as friends, family member or an acquaintance either one of you will have to send a "friend request" to the other and have the request accepted. The technology then recognises you as "friends" and you can communicate with each other online; you can also view the other person's profile detail, pictures, and send them messages as well.

Safety

This is one aspect of social media a lot of users do not really pay attention to. Most fail to see the dangers inherent in using these platforms. Generally speaking, almost all the interactions that take place on social media are quite safe. Nevertheless, you should be conscious of your safety and the information about yourself you share. It important for everyone using social media to remember these safety tips:

1. You do not have to accept a friend request from a user you do not know or would rather not want to be in contact with.

2. Do your best to take into consideration the privacy of other users when putting up photos or videos of them, or mentioning them in posts where other users might read about it.

3. Also worthy of note is the fact that you can remove someone as a friend and also block them from interacting with you even after you have accepted their friend request if you are not pleased with their actions online, especially if those actions puts you at risk.

4. You might as well adjust your privacy settings so that only your family and friends can view your profile page and communicate with you.

Children and parents/wards

Every parent should try to encourage open dialogue with their kids and teenagers about what their activities online by inquiring of them which social media platforms they are currently on. Parents could also sign up and create their own profile as a good way to get to know how social media works.

Most popular social media sites in brief

Much later in this publication we'd look deep at popular social media sites and what they are about but here is a brief of some of the most popular sites out there:

Facebook is a social networking site that enables people from the world over to interact with their family, friends, companies and organizations.

Instagram is a social networking site that allows users to upload and share pictures and short videos using their mobile device or PCs.

LinkedIn is a business-related social networking site that is used mainly by professionals to connect with other professionals in their industry.

Pinterest is a unique social networking site that lets users upload, organize, and share information using virtual "pin-boards".

Tumblr is a blogging site which allows users to post text, images, videos, links, quotes and audio.

Twitter is the popular micro-blogging site that lets people to post short updates that contain 140 characters or less.

YouTube is currently the world's largest video sharing site that allows users to create channels where they upload and organize video contents and amass subscribers.

CHAPTER TWO

THE WORLD AND LIFESTYLE BEFORE THE EVOLUTION OF SOCIAL MEDIA

It is a very herculean task for me to remember what life was like before social media, and I am quite old (...twenty-something). If you are above 25 years of age you might have a small glimpse of what life was like before social media came along. However, for teenager it is nearly impossible to.

But let's face it guys, there actually was a time before the internet, a time before all the media buzz, the like buttons, the tweets, the viral posts, etc. in this chapter we are going to take a trip back in time, with a literary "wayback" (ever seen Mr. Peabody?)

It is evident that life has changed so drastically over the past decade that it's nearly impossible for any teenager these days to comprehend **how**

anybody ever survived without a constant internet connection. As a matter of fact, it sounds weird to us now to actually bring to mind how we spent our time back then, although the memories still linger. If I had to tell it in one word the first memory I have about life before the Internet, I would choose "**quiet**". And I don't mean a literal "quiet", it's rather metaphorical, as it was, like I said before, devoid of all media buzz we deal with presently. Like it or not, communication before the internet and social media was more personal, and intimate (in my own words) and face-to-face contact was a lot **less awkward**. Even as a child, playing and studying was markedly different, were group games such as scrabble, chess, snake and ladder, hide and seek (it probably went by a different name where you come from), etc took place on the playground, and real hardcover encyclopaedias were used as a medium to find the information you needed.

Here's how we (some of us above 25) and our parents did some things before the emergence of social media:

- **We had face-to-face meetings whenever we had a group projects. Since** there was no Face-time or Google Docs or Facebook to make physical meetings totally unnecessary, we had to ask all the difficult and awkward questions in person.

- **We actually went to physical libraries and consulted actual books to get answers to a simple question. Sadly then** there was no Google to give us the answers we sought.

- **And when we went to a library, we sort for books (amongst a thousand others) utilizing a filing system with thousands of index cards (Dewey Decimal system).** We had no computers to look up the book titles (or get a map to the book's precise location).

- **We used newspapers to get the news of the day. While** now there's YouTube and Twitter to get all the most up-to-date news on the spot, newspapers are currently used for arts and crafts projects at school.

- **We had to use actual paper maps and atlases to get from point A to point B and to know where USA is on the planet, respectively.** There weren't GPS's or smart phones equipped with Google Maps to tell us *precisely* where to go... and where not to.

- **During daylights savings we had to manually turn back the hands of time... oh, I mean the hands of our clocks.** No digital settings automatically changed our clocks back.

- **They (our parents) wrote their school papers using huge computers the size of cathode ray TVs.** There weren't laptops back then.

- **Quite interestingly we couldn't stalk our crush secretly.** In the absence of Instagram, Facebook, Twitter or Google, garnering intel on your crush was a lot harder and required more skill.

- **We literally had to call people on the phone. And** missing out on class required top-notch acting skills. We couldn't send our teachers emails at the last minute with our paper attached explaining to them how we were too ill to make it to class. We were forced to call and try to pretend to be sick on the phone.

- **No online shopping, no Amazon or eBay.** We ordered clothes (and other things) by filling out some forms from catalogues and then sending them off in the mail with a check. It usually took anywhere from a few weeks to MONTHS for orders to come in. Yes, you read that correctly - MONTHS!

- **Back then we had to politely other peoples' opinions or concepts.** And that's because long before Facebook and the YouTube comments section existed, we had to express our opinions in person instead of behind faceless profiles.

- **When there was nothing to for us to do, we had to find something somewhat "productive-ish" to do.** In other words, when we had no friends to hang out with, or anywhere fun to go like the cinema, or WWE arena, we were forced to do things like read, write, paint, exercise, or other productive things like that which many today would consider boring.

What communication was like long before social media (Overview)

Communication could quite appropriately be tagged "the motor that keeps the world turning". From the beginning of life forms on this blue rock called earth there has been several modes of communication between every living thing. The history of communication exposes numerous ways through which we communicated as we continually sought knowledge to add to them.

But really have you ever thought about the history of human communication? It is a very captivating journey back in time - to a prehistoric start when man blew animal horns and banged drums. The introduction of fire facilitated beacons and smoke signals to be sent across significant distances. I can somewhat estimate that in the fifth century an "airmail" system was devised by the use of pigeons, hawks, and kites. The fourth century saw the advent of the hydraulic telegraph system developed by the Grecians. It actually involved sending of signals illuminated by fire and was restricted to only "line of sight" distance.

After that and prior to the telegraph and telephone the major means of communication between people other than face-to-face conversation was 'letter writing'. People wrote letters in much the same way you and I would have a conversation over a voice call on a phone. Evidently the contents spanned from a simple 'hi', 'hello', 'how are you?' to very formal documents. Although literacy rates shot up very quickly throughout the nineteenth century, people who couldn't read or write simply sought assistance from someone in their family or immediate community. What almost every historian (and me) always finds interesting is how letter writing was nearly an art. While the aesthetics of the handwriting enriched even the most unexciting of contents, the shear passion with which these personal letters were written clearly showed the value people put upon the letter. While in high school, despite the fact that smart phones were already in vogue, I handwrote letters to some of my love interests, and believe me it was fun.

Technology at the time of letter writing was restricted to pretty much a "pen", commonly a quill feather that had to be sharpened by cutting, and paper, a costly substance at that time due to the nature of its production process, there were also different grades available (cheaper, lower quality paper was more susceptible to decay, and had more pulp, amongst other features that showed low quality). Writing in those days was as well considered an evidence of education and status. A lot of letters were sent from one point to another for many different reasons and by individuals from all walks of life. However, in the mid-1800's, new advances would be made that would go to revolutionize the way people communicated.

The first genuine way to communicate with people across significant distances that didn't involve the mail service was invented sometime around 1828. The telegraph then was a very crude device that poked dots and tore dashes into paper to be translated at the receiving end. Think of this as the fore-runner of texting. 1830 saw notable advancements as a message was sent over one mile.

Modes of communication back then and how they worked

Okay don't get this twisted, this isn't a communication history book; there are plenty of those on the internet already. But for you and me to really appreciate social media in all its glory, glamour, and grandeur we have to go down to the past, to the very cusp of the stone-age. The need to communicate has been the driving force to much development in the entire human history, and more so the need to communicate over distances too long to shout over has been just as essential. Let's start from one of the earliest, most noteworthy form of communication:

Yelling

At a certain point in human communication history, to communicate over a distance a person had to yell, which was pretty cool at the time; it was quite cost effective; all you needed was a mouth, a pair of lungs, and a belly full of food. And they were getting pretty good at it I tell you. Ever wondered how generals addressed their troops numbering in the tens of thousands on an open field on a windy day?

Blowing horns and bugles also communicated messages over great distances that yelling couldn't cover. For example, troops used the bugle largely to communicate orders to troops. However, it was not to last: as the distance grew they quickly found out that there was only so much yelling and honking one could do. Plus, it could quickly give away a person's position... especially to wild animals. Therefore man had to come up with something brilliant:

Smoke/fire Signals

Don't get me wrong, it was good (and cheap) to yell away your message at your friend half a kilometre away, however, it got old fast, and it became more and more vital to communicate rapidly such as when a battalion of soldiers needed to swoop in to save their compatriots, or a government needed to stop a war entirely... or start one, and so sending messengers was too slow and tedious; and to communicate over more than shouting, or direct line-of-sight, distances; for instance, a government, say the ancient Romans, trying to stop its troops from fighting a perceived enemy... or from peeing into the city's main drinking water supply. Then came smoke/fire signals.

The smoke signal is one of the most archaic forms of long-distance communication. It is a visual form of communication used over long distance. Smoke signalling mainly involved generating a draft of smoke with a fire and a wet blanket from a high elevation, such as a hill, so everyone close enough could see the cloud of smoke rising into the air. In general smoke signals were used to convey news, warn about impending danger, or gather the locals to the village square. In ancient China, soldiers positioned along the famous Great Wall would inform each other of impending enemy attack by signalling from tower to tower. Using this, they were able to send a message as far away as a whopping 750 kilometres in a mere matter of hours.

Sadly, history has it that the abuse of the smoke/fire signal is implicated in the fall of the Western Zhou Dynasty in the 8th century BC. King You (no, I don't mean you, the reader) of Zhou had a bad habit of deceiving his warlords with phony warning beacons in order to amuse his side chick, Bao Si, who at the time was known as one of four ancient hotties of China. And when an actual rebellion happened, nobody came to the aid of the king. Talk about a severe case of "crying wolf".

Polybius, a Greek historian (a smart guy, I guess), came up with a more byzantine system of alphabetical smoke signals sometime around 150

BC, his system converted Greek alphabetic characters into numeric characters. It allowed messages to be easily transmitted by holding sets of torches in pairs. This idea, later came to be known as the "Polybius square", and is the precursor to cryptography and steganography. This cryptographic concept has been used as well with Japanese Hiragana and the Germans in the following years of the World War II. The North American indigenous peoples also communicated via smoke signal. Every tribe had its peculiar signalling code and arrangement.

Writing and Letters

In its crudest form, writing as a means of communication involved basic forms or symbols impressed on cave walls in prehistoric times. Slowly but steadily, writing systems grew and evolved as people continued in their passion to communicate with one another. Almost every culture created and developed its own alphabetic and numerical scripts engraved on wooden or stone slab. Ultimately, the paper was invented, and written communication took an incredible step forward as several people began to gain the ability to scribble on this new portable surface.

The United States Postal Service has grown and developed in significant ways since its beginning at the foundation of the country. In the beginning, its service was quite inconsistent based on where the offices were located. Mail bearers had to journey over tedious (and dangerous) routes, even routes hundreds of miles long, devoid of modern roads and usually on foot. Consequentially, not every part of the US benefitted from the postal service, even in the beginning of the 19th century. Mail travelled across the country either on foot, by horse or mule, and on inland waterways. The introduction of the transcontinental railroad system in 1869 gave the mail service a massive boost, with letters moving from coast-to-coast in a week or less.

Therefore, letter writing replaced smoke signals as a means of communication. Everyone back then wrote letters to keep in touch with family and friends broken up by distance as it was the only way to communicate over long distances, at least until the arrival of the telegraph in the 19th century.

Printing press

The writing mode of communication blew up massively with the invention of paper. And with its invention the print revolution was born, in the East. Although by the turn of the eighth century, most likely earlier, printing had already been carried out in China. A technique called "block printing" which made use of a carved block made of wood to print a page of certain text on a material (such as paper) was the most commonplace. And then in 1450Johann Gutenberg invented a printing press in the west that would print with metal type. Printing proliferated throughout Europe, leading to the creation of books and newspapers as well. (Briggs and Burke 13-14).

The telegraph

The telegraph had been in development since 1684 starting with the optical telegraph. And from then on, several inventors had come up with their own versions, amongst whom are: Richard Lovell Edgeworth, the Chappe brothers, Samuel Thomas von Sömmering, Francisco SalvaCampillo, Francis Ronalds, Pavel Schilling, Carl Friedrich Gauss and Wilhelm Weber, William Fothergill Cooke and Charles Wheatstone, Samuel Morse, Alfred Vail (Morse's assistant), Edward Davy. However, Samuel F.B Morse independently invented an electric telegraph in the US which sent messages using a set of dots and dashes, that later came to be known as the Morse code.

The telegraph functioned by sending messages using electrical pulses that travelled through wires. The Morse code made up the messages which are entered by the sender pressing down a key on the machine. The recipient on the other end would need to be able to decipher the Morse code in order to make sense of its content. Morse already laid out the three component of the telegraph which includes the sender, the receiver and the code itself. The telegraph worked thus: the sender would open and close the electric circuit, the receiver then used the electromagnet to record the transmitted signal, and the code rendered the signals into alphanumeric symbols.

In just 10 years, well over 20 thousand miles of telegraph broadcast links had crossed the nation. This expansion made it feasible for different types of quick correspondence. The telegraph genuinely changed the world in light of the fact that before broadcasts, the nation was cut-off from the other parts of the world. Suffice to say, the telegraph was the first major breakthrough in the evolution of mass communication technology as it spearheaded many of the devices we use presently and being that it used similar techniques to what we use nowadays. Extension in this preceding technology paved way for many of the inventions we use today, including telephones, radio, cable TV, Internet, and cell phones.

Telephone

And so it wasn't too long after the telegraph took over as the major mass communication medium before the next big break in technology came along - the telephone! The telephone works byconverting sound to electricity and back again. It was also based on electrical systems that made use of wires, just like the telegraph, and this contributed to its success. Unfortunately, it failed to carry signals under-water as the water interfered with the flow of electricity, drastically reducing its strength. Hence, it could not be used intercontinentally.

Nevertheless, AT&T came up with solution; they made cables that consisted of steel wires (later copper became more mainstream because it conducts electricity better) insulated by plastic jackets. The plastic jackets or "armour" shielded the flow of current from external factors, such as moisture; thereby allowing interrupted transmission. This innovation in cable technology greatly enhanced the transmitted signals leading to the establishment of telephone systems in homes, thus connecting the entire world with just a pair of copper wires cables installed on poles delivering telephone service to homes. This innovation also led to the birth of cable TV and cell phones.

The Internet

Fast forward about a hundred years after the invention of the telephone, and something was born which would take over the planet's mode of communication, and change our lives forever – the internet!

The Internet unofficially began in the 1960s; it was created to help government researchers and scientists share information among themselves. Because of the large and clunky computers that were used at the time one had to travel to the location of the machine that had the information they wanted, or have a magnet tape sent over containing the desired data – unlike laptops today, moving these computers wasn't an option. They weight like 1600olbs and used about 5000 vacuum tubes.

Funny enough, one factor also credited with influencing the creation of the internet was the famous Cold War. The US DOD, motivated by the Soviet's launch of Sputnik, began to contemplate way through which information could be sent in the event that the US was nuked. This path led to the creation of the Advanced Research Projects Agency Network, also called ARPANET. And it was a huge accomplishment, even though its use was restricted to research institutes who had dealings with the Department of Defence and a few academic bodies. Subsequently, other networks were formed to provide sharing of information.

In January 1, 1983 the Internet was officially born. Before this time, all computer networks did not communicate with each other in a standard way. Then a novel communications protocol was established termed Transfer Control Protocol/Internetwork Protocol or TCP/IP (I'm sure you've come across that somewhere). This enables various types of computers on separate networks to communicate. Therefore, all networks were connected by a universal language.

Email

The birth of the internet and the commercialization of computers opened up an entire world of possibilities. Communication began to grow exponentially, at unprecedented levels and the world was now more connected than it had ever been. One thing that resulted from this growth was the Electronic mail, popularly called Email. The email allows people to create, send and receive, and store electronic letters on their computers.

And with emailing things began to get more interesting, and gradually the world of communication edged steadily towards social media. Following the email are:

Chat Rooms

Chat rooms grew in popularity over several years, as it at one time was the primary style of Internet communication. Issues with web safety and appropriate topics of discussion gave chat rooms a bad reputation later in its development cycle. Nonetheless, chat rooms made a small but crucial transition into what we have as social media today.

Instant Messaging

Instant messaging was a rave (I remember) when it came on board. I vividly remember the time when I couldn't wait to get to my PC to get on Yahoo chat – it was an exciting time. Though it still remains till this day it hasn't changed in its core form, and IM is major web communication method. Today we have its equivalent as Whatsapp, and Facebook chat, amongst others.

Forums

Forums are platforms that allow people with similar interests to come together to discuss topical issues and concerns. They popularized the term "Thread" which describes a long series of messages posted by different members of the forum. Forums have remained largely unchanged since their inception, even in the face of the current social media boom. Evidently, social media sites, such as Facebook, have adopted the use of forum-styled boards have left them unmodified with regards to functionality. Today's social media equivalent of forum include: blackhatworld, Facebook discussions, etc.

CHAPTER THREE

Definition of Social Media

Do you often think that social media is just all about posting status updates and comments on Facebook? Well, you are not alone. Facebook doesn't totally define the concept of social media and is still one of the most popular, if not the most popular, and influential platforms. Social media has expanded to become a medium for personal and also professional interactions and has evolved to include many solid web platforms and tools.

When someone says "social media", I can bet the first thing that popped into your head was a picture of your Facebook wall, or Twitter homepage, Instagram feed, or Youtube channel, right? Sure, it is. As you may have already garnered from chapter one, Facebook, Twitter, Instagram, Youtube aren't the only social media platforms out there on the net, in spite of the fact that they have long been topping the social media industry.

The point is, social media is much more than the big four listed in the paragraph above and so defining what social media is quite difficult. In order to help you get a clear understanding of what social media really is, here's a definition derived from the perspective of several industry experts, lexicologists, business men and women, and everyday social media users. At the end of this section, you'll have an all-encompassing idea of what social media is, and what it's not.

Here's what Social media is:

Social media is primarily a computer-mediated, internet based applications and tools (that can also be accessed through cellular phones and tabs)that allows people to share information amongst themselves. It comprises renowned networking platforms, like Facebook and Twitter; video sharing sites like Youtube and Instagram; as well as bookmarking sites like Reddit. Others also include Pintrest, LinkedIn,

Tumblr, etc. Also included are forums and blogging and any form of interactive presence that avails users the ability to hold conversations with each other, privately (through inboxes), or publicly (through threads) which can lead to the formation of communities of users with similar interests, and new relationships on a personal level.

So let's take a look at those features that are shared by most, if not all, social media platforms:

Common features of social media

Participation

Every social media platform out there encourages contributions and feedback from its users, making the line between audience and media very blurred.

Openness

Virtually all social media services are receptive to feedback and participation. They also urge users to vote, comment, like, and share information. It isn't common to find restrictions to accessing and making use of shared content.

Conversation

Unlike traditional media where content broadcasted to an audience, social media is sort of like a two-way conversation between the media and its audience.

Community

One of the major features of Social media is its ability to bring large number of people together to form communities that interact online. They are made up of people with shared interests like gaming, science, business, etc.

Connectedness

Most social media flourish on their being able to link to other related resources, sites, individuals, etc.

Reason for the invention of Social media

In the history of communication, and the internet one can effortlessly place a finger on ground-breaking accomplishments such as who invented the telegraph, or the first telephone call, or first email sent, and can easily duff our hats for these guys for their great contribution to our society. However, it's a whole different kettle of fish when you consider Social media in the light of 'who invented it'. By the way, who the hell puts fishes in a kettle? That's weird.

Okay, if we are to consider it from the aspect of the pioneering technologies that can be termed as 'social media', then the credit for the invention of Social Media should go to no other than Tom Truscott and Jim Ellis who in 1979 (or so) created the world's first usenet systems. Usenets allowed users to create, post, and read messages from several categories, known then as "newsgroups". In our present reality, they can be thought of as a crossbreed between email and web forums; and a lot of other popular group sites we have today, including Google Groups and Yahoo! Groups, as well as RSS feeds are all fundamentally based on these technologies.

I could say that fundamentally Social media was invented by our crushing need to communicate quickly, effectively, and with as many people as possible. Coming through communication history, as we have done in the previous chapter, you can see that at every timeline in our history we have always sort ways to communicate, to reach out to one another without any barrier of distance or climate. We are social creatures, and when we seek and come up with media to talk to one another without constraints, interesting concepts are born.

How Social media became a global means of communication

Actually it was improvement in web publishing tech and the sole concept of allowing front-end users to have access to publishing tools available to only back-ends of Content Management Systems (CMS) that initially empowered Social media. However, here are four other crucial factors that led to its explosion.

- **Broadband**

Hey anyone remember trying to view images on your browser with 70 kb/s dial up internet connection? Yeah, I know what it was like: almost like a snail trying to win the Grand Turismo.

Massive improvement in broadband infrastructure from the year 2000, which enhanced download and upload speeds, made Social media gizmos more accessible and easier to use.

- **Cloud computing**

Cloud computing has made social media usability very easy by stashing heavy digital content in what is called 'cloud storage systems'. Because Videos and pictures, even audio files are the most common content on social media, it can quickly fill up the amount of storage space allocated to each user, consequently causing the entire system to drag making user experience terrible. Cloud storage shares the weight and takes the load off the Social media platform allowing it to run smoothly thus enhancing user experience.

Besides data storage, the social media networks are using clouds computing for other very important tasks as well, such as data analysis. One of the merits of working with cloud systems is that Social media owners and users have access enormous amount of structured (even non-structured) data easily. You might understand better if you look at tools like google analytics used by millions of Social media platform owner to track movement and activities on their sites.

- **Mobile Internet**

Prior to the year 2009 not many smart phone were out on the open market and the only way to access the internet at the time was through a desktop or laptop computers, which not many people owned at the time. And so these limitations in internet access reduced online communication. However, in the wake of high-tech smart phones, mobile browsing platforms, WiFi connectivity, and stable data network, one could access social media at any time with just a few swipes, and could also spend as much time as possible on there.

- **In-built 'virality'**

The advent of online features like a 'share', 'like', 'retweet' and more recently 'clap' meant that contents on social media could spread amongst several thousand people anywhere from a few hours to a few weeks. Many Social media platforms now employ these tools to keep their membership skyrocketing and this is because word of mouth is the best form of marketing;

you'd be more willing to watch a video or read a post if recommended by a friend than otherwise. And so this built-in virality tools help Social media to grow in popularity much more rapidly.

Chapter four

Effects of Social media

Social media has become a crucial piece of our society today. It somehow has become the structure upon which our present society is built given the amount of information being distributed everyday over different platforms. They children are the leaders of tomorrow and this statement holds true as far as social media is concerned; we can catch a glimpse of social media will be in years to come by looking at how they interact with it and how it affects them now. Spending an average of 6 hours daily on social media, according to reports, it is clearly evident that this tool is bound to have very significant effects on the lives of our youths.

Despite the fact that social media has is inherent ills and dangers, such as identity theft, depression, amongst a host of others, it also has its good side. Social media has been the source of many happy endings, innovations, helps, etc. which if applied appropriately will continue to change our society for good.

If you continue reading you'd see how social media has impacted our youths and how it continues to. And if you are reading this as a youth I'm quite sure you can relate with at least one or two of these points:

POSITIVE EFFECTS OF SOCIAL MEDIA
Staying in touch

If you have family, relatives, or friends who reside far from you, say in the village, a different state, or even another country, social media serves as a great medium to connect and stay connected with them for as long as you want without making long phones calls. You may do this by sending them pictures, chatting them up, making video calls (which rocks, by the way), and voice messages. In time past it was tedious to keep in touch will people once they aren't within your immediate vicinity or, even harder, country but social media has helped to bring the world together, making communication very easy even in absence.

Education

Social media is a great resource for learning. The bible says, "In the last days knowledge shall increase..." I'm in no doubt it was referring in part to social media. Young people use social media to pick up skills they may not be able to get in their local area. And for teachers, social media can be used to reach more people. You can hand out flyers on your street and run radio ads and have an attendance of a few hundred people however, with social media you can draw a much larger audience numbering in the hundreds of thousands, even millions. Just look at the amount of traffic certain channels on Youtube pull. The Avengers: Infinity Wars trailer had a whopping 50 million views in just two weeks. There are online education sites that give out valuable courses for free and have up to 4 million users e.g. Allison, Lynda, Thenewboston, etc.

Save Time and Money

Unlike yester years when you had to go out to get or do almost everything, with the advent of social media a person can garner information without going to the library or bookshop; you can earn a degree (even masters) in the comfort of your home through distance learning programmes. You can make purchases through ads on Facebook, Youtube, Instagram, and even on Twitter without going to the department store.

To voice opinion

Several social media platforms such as Facebook, instagram, and Twitter are currently being harnessed by both young and old to speak for those who cannot speak for themselves. Currently on Facebook, and other platforms like Twitter, for example, tags like "stop slavery in Lybia" and "Blacks are not for sale" are being share to make society more aware of the on-going slavery of migrants in Lybia. A lot of these campaigns are instigated by young people who recognize the evil in slavery and importance of human rights and treating everyone equally regardless of their race, and social media serves as the perfect tool to spread that awareness.

Making Friends

Of course, this remains the most important positive effect of social media platforms that anyone reading this article can relate to, and my list is incomplete without it. It is a hell of a lot easier to make friends presently than it was several decades ago. For shy people, making friends is a lot less awkward and much more fun with just a click of a button, they do not need to go out and start the nerve-racking process of striking a conversation with a total stranger.

Today, thanks to social media, connecting with total stranger is completely easy, and it's very possible to make thousands of friends on sites like Facebook or Twitter, even though they might not be very friends like those you can share personal information with, whatever, they are still friends, and someday one or two of them could turn out to be the best of friends you've ever had.

Creativity and innovation

Social media sites thrive on active, real-time involvement in creation and sharing of different content. This causes young people think outside the box on their toes (okay, not literally though) and produce fresh new content when disseminating information. And with this new apps and sites are born every other day, showing newer ways to portray creativity.

Empathy

People tend to use social media to express their misfortune or feelings or mistakes. Well, they have different reasons why they do this; some find relief because "a problem shared is a problem half-solved", others do it to seek empathy from others who may be going or have gone through the same ordeal. They will read what was posted and assist in any way they can in dealing with the issues you are battling.

The fact here is, as we all share bad (and good) experiences on social media, we can show empathy to each other.

Skill acquisition

People, with the help of social media, are more than ever able to communicate freely and effortlessly in various online social environments, just like they do in real life in their place of work. This is the direct result of the unending exposure and experience they garner from being constantly online and conversing with different people, from all over the globe, some of whom may be potential employers. Young, and old, people procure skills that allow them to analyse and understand diverse situations per time and make themselves mentally ready for those situations later in life. YouTube particularly, but now Facebook and Instagram, have hundreds of thousands of skill acquisition videos that can give anyone who is willing the ability to hone and develop their different skills and talents. One can learn to play the piano, design websites and apps, write codes, and even cook.

Self-confidence and independence

Social networking sites serves as an exciting experience and afresh adventure for young and even old people. Just like exploring a new place where different skills are required. Social media helps people learn to build character to be a lot more confident and independent if they want to be heard or have a positive impact online with their presence. This process ultimately transfers to their daily lives offline.

And let's not forget this bit..

Job Opportunities:

Social media is a great tool for professionals for marketing, networking, and seeking new business opportunities. Employers also find qualified employees and unemployed folks have been able to find work online. A whopping 89% of job recruiters have hired through LinkedIn, 26% used Facebook, and 15% via Twitter. Social media sites have created millions of new jobs and new sources of income.

Now that's something, isn't it?

NEGATIVE EFFECTS OF SOCIAL MEDIA

Okay, that's all nice and good, boohoos, I'm crying in my seat already about how beneficial social media is to our society and the world at large, however, life is not a bed of roses, and with good always comes evil. As much as mass improvement in communication technology has had very significant positive impact in our lives, we cannot deny the fact that it came with its truckload of ills. Here we are going to look at a few of them, which I'm quite can all relate to, either directly or indirectly. So, let's dig in, shall we?

Addiction

That is a fact! Social media can be very addictive. Want to know how addicted you already are? Ask yourself this question: How long can you stay away from every form of social media, assuming you could get all the information you need offline, without losing your sanity? Or how long can you stay with a mobile device or without connection to the internet without feeling like you are missing your kidneys? I'm sure you know your answer to any of those questions. People spend hours and hours on social media, reading posts, comments, liking or reacting to posts and comments, playing games, or working, so much so that it's extremely difficult for them stay away without feeling like they are going to die, or worse. A lot of folks out there particularly cannot stay away from their mobile phones, tabs, or computers.

Reduced Productivity

Today, with a lot of companies and businesses using social media to source for and commune with potential customers, these platforms are also a great source of distraction to worker who most likely show more interest in what their friends online are sharing than their work and as a direct consequence, they will be a lot less productive than normal. Though new technology products have been invented that allow social media networks to be blocked in offices, still they are very ineffective.

Lack of Privacy

A lot of people out there, particularly the young ones, are often unnecessarily open and unguarded with their personal information when they are online. Many do not read privacy policies of these platforms (Okay, I confess I've never read any website's policy without falling asleep, still...) and may not be aware that such information may and can be used by unwanted third parties, like advertisers, insurance companies, thieves, and worse - the IRS! Over 21% of teenagers think it's safe and unhazardous to post personal details on social media, including photos, location, and even financial information. This exposes them to corporate and governmental incursion. Careless habits like these help the US Justice Department to intercepts thousands of pieces of information from private emails and social media activities per year. The IRS isn't slacking either; they train their agents to be able to scan social media for details that can help tackle taxpayer issues. Insurance companies also use information garnered from social media sites. If you have ever clicked the "like" button of any notable medical-related page or a post concerning a health condition, that singular act is sometimes interpreted by insurance companies to ascertain eligibility and increase their rates.

Have it in mind that online advertising policies are an invasion of privacy, and whenever you "like" a brand/product; you're automatically giving access to your private information to that company.

Cyber-Bullying

In recent years of social media reign, cyber-bullying has become a prominent issue for young people. The same speed of access supplied by social media platforms is available to the good, the bad, and others. Online attacks not properly handled could leave deep emotional scars, and lead to depression, loss of self-esteem, and even suicide. The obscurity given online could tempt people to express some dark desires which may otherwise be dormant. Cyber-bullying is quite common among youngster in these days.

Isolation

Okay, this might sound like an oxymoron: the thing that brings people together isolates them. Yep, it sure does. However, there's nothing truer than this. Social media really does pull people together forming online forums and communities were interests are shared, but at the same time, behind the scene, it causes social isolation. People now spend a huge fraction of their day on social media, thereby spending less and less time with real people in real life. Scientists have been assessing social isolation in several studies, and have ascertained that it could result in a change unphysical, psychological, and emotional issues, such as depression, anxiety, aggression, and many others. As a matter of fact, social isolation can significantly mar production of certain brain hormones, which is the reason why socially isolated people exhibit heightened levels of stress, anxiety, and aggression. Some brain disorders such as ADHD, narcissistic tendencies, a need for immediate gratification, and addictive behaviours (like alcoholism) and other emotional distress like depression and loneliness.

Spend More Money

It is implied in several researches that heavy social media use may be more correlated to lower financial self-control than we are willing to admit; and these, marketing experts believe, will result in higher spending. We all know how easy it is click that "add to cart' button under that cool Nike shoe, or that red dress (for prom, if anyone still attends such), or that piece of jewellery, and have it delivered to your doorstep without you leaving your chair. This easy of purchase makes spending less controlled and online store owners and designers know this and are looking for more ways to make it even easier. Ultimately, the best way to counteract this is by increasing their self-discipline and financial planning.

Exposure to Crime

A sad but true thing is that social media avail hate groups to employ and distribute misleading information online.

Illegal distribution and uncontrolled copyright infringement seriously threatens intellectual property online and also causes massive loss of income.

Security issues such as identity theft, phishing scams, hacking, and viruses are widespread online. Nearly 68% of users permit people to know their actual birth date; another 63% share the name of their high school and tertiary institutions, and even their qualifications; over 18% give out their telephone numbers, and 12% share their pet's name. The catch? These details can be used by unscrupulous individuals to steal one's identity.

Criminals can and have used social media to perpetrate crimes. Robbers can find out when you're not home, maybe on a vacation or at work, and stalkers also glean information of your location through social media. Sexual predators seek, stalk, and assail victims using information gotten from social media.

Texting sexual content, known as "Sexting" is a rapidly growing concern for a lot of people. When people upload sexually related photos or comments on social media, it can result to the user having criminal charges dropped on them and lead to child pornography as well. Over 88% of "personal" sexual photographs uploaded to social media are taken and publicly used on pornography sites... of course, without the subject's knowledge or consent.

A Waste of Time

When notified about a new update, tweet, or video up load (for Youtube and Instagram) it usually takes about 20 to 25 minutes (longer for some others) for the average social media user to go back to the original task they were running. And 30% of the time it may require up to two hours for the user to return to their original task.

Alter the Appetite

Okay, I know this is weird. What has food got to do with social media, right? As cheesy as this might sound it is quite a valid point. Widely known as "food porn" i.e. photographs of food is capable of altering the program of the brain's reward centre thereby causing a person to over eat. Research has proven that staring at pictures of meals could set off hunger in people.

There are so many other negative effects social media has on its users but these ones already listed should give you an idea. Feel free to add yours. The truth is most of this negative effects can be avoided if only users can apply some discretion and discipline. Go to the concluding page to know more about using social media without having to deal with the ills.

Chapter five

How social media is used to control human mind

Yeah, this might be a lot difficult to take in, and it sure sounds like something out of a sci-fi movie. The thing is if you feel strongly against this concept chances are they have already got you by the "nuts". Without any elaborate research any 6 year-old with a smart phone would have noticed by now that lures online, especially on social media that subtly urges you give out more of your information. That eggs you on to choose something "related" to a previous site you just visited. As helpful as this may seem on the surface, there are powers that track and gather information left by users on social media as they navigate through posts, comments, links, etc. For every time a user "likes" or "shares" or "comments" on a topic on threads, he/she leaves an impression that data miners use to ascertain that persons political or religious stance; buying choices; entertainment preferences, emotional type, and so on. Using IP and GPS tracking, the collective mind of a particular geographic area can mapped and that information can then be used spread propaganda, and manipulate the choices of the people in that area.

This is currently going on as you read this book, and been going on for years long before the internet was born. Social media is only a 21st century tool that used for an agenda that was hatched long before some of our parents were born. The goal of many social media is to draw in as many people, and keep them on there for as long as possible, knowing that the longer they stay on the platform the more addicted they'll become, and the more addicted they become the more likely they'll believe what is on there. It makes it even better through friendship, because it's easier to get on a platform if your friend is already there. Like I said earlier in this book, social media is word of mouth on steroids. When an item is shared online it spreads through relationships. You are most likely to support a course if your friends online support it, and are most likely going to disregard what your friends disregard.

For hundreds of centuries, almost since the recordable history of mankind, there has always been a small but powerful group of people who believe they had to control the 'masses' one way or another, to their own selfish interests. They have always represented no more than 5% of the entire population of the world. Back in medieval times, and prior to that, this was achieved through sheer force, military force. The group, or region, or country with the most powerful military force controlled the will of the lesser. History holds records of countries that have at one time been world power such as Babylon, Egypt, Rome, Persia, etc. they all achieved dominance through military might.

Military force couldn't and didn't have the kind of results they hoped to get, although at the time it was enough; wars cost money, and someday somehow some group somewhere would rise from the ashes, and topple the world power.

As knowledge grew, man devised means of mass communication, to be able to reach a large number of people at the same time. And again there's always the small 'elite' group who'd take advantage of such media to manipulate the minds of the general populace. Where military might fail, print media worked magic. Back when print media became the major medium of communication, a well-tailored propaganda could spread panic much more than a thousand soldiers and armored tanks could. These set of people used it as a weapon to make the general populace do their bidding without so much as showing their faces. As soft weapon, I'd say.

In 1914, a propaganda caused by the outbreak of war, is regarded as the first large-scale propaganda orchestrated by any government. Certain German military officials (including Erich Ludendorff and Adolf Hitler) believed that such propaganda contributed greatly to the

British victory. Before that, in the era of the Reformation, propaganda helped the spread of new doctrines, ideology, and beliefs at unprecedented levels across Europe than had ever been witnessed before. During the American revolution, propaganda also spread across the colonies. And these three instances were achieved using print media.

Then came the radio, and with it information could travel faster than it could on print media. And history is riddled with instances were radio propaganda was used to manipulate the minds and emotions of the general populace to act in a certain way. Same thing happened with the invention of TV, movies, video games, etc.

In as much as that still happens in our day and time the medium through which it is achieved has changed, dramatically. Social media packs the control-power of all the previous media, and more... much more.

Social media is a lot more effective for certain reasons: the improvement in technology with devices like smartphones makes social media easily accessible, anytime, anywhere; unlike the other forms of mass communication which just beamed information at its audience in a one-way stream, social media is a two-way communication medium, allowing instantaneous transfer of information from source to audience and vice-versa; social media taps into peer-influence in the way that other previous media could not; social combines the power of text, digital images and video, and voice all in one, making older mass communication tools lame.

As I mentioned earlier, large amounts of data is collected over social media and this information is analysed and then used to understand and manipulate the state of mind and decisions of users. In 2010, Facebook conducted an experiment during a congressional election to test the ability of the platform to influence the voting decisions of its users. The results were astounding. Over 60,000 people were directly influenced by the test message to go out and vote; another 280,000 people were influenced indirectly, through social contagion or peer-influence, bring the total to a whopping 340,000 people, who would have otherwise not voted. That figure was 0.14% of the US voting-age population which at the time was 236million.

(Go here to read full article and other resources to get more information:https://www.huffingtonpost.com/jeremy-lent/the-new-mind-manipulators_b_9760268.html**)**

Also visit: *https://newint.org/blog/2016/03/11/google-and-facebook-flip-elections-code-rules-the-world*

Ever heard of the term CAPTOLOGY? Let me explain: Captology come from the acronym CAPT, meaning Computer As a Persuasive Technology, and so Captology is the study of computer as a persuasive technology. Believe me, this is an actual course which has it base at the Persuasive Tech Lab, at Stanford University, with B.J Fogg as its Director. On the surface these studies are said to be done to help the masses communicate better using computers as a medium however, certain recent trends are showing that that isn't the case at all. This year, Facebook openly declared its intention to build a mind-control section of its platform, and Google is in on it too.

Blown yet?

Follow the links I provided and read up more materials on the subject and you will be amazed at what's going on behind your computer screens through social media. If you still don't believe it (for your sake I hope you do) then there's almost nothing anyone can do for you.

Chapter six

The way out

The world is a more connected place thanks to social media. Evidently, it has brought a lot of great things with it. For example, you can share (positive) information to thousands; even millions of people in an instant or you can learn a new skill which can significantly improve your earnings or you can reconnect with long lost friends or relatives with a click of the button or you promote your business or company in the face of thousands of potential customers. Incredible things! However, as with everything else it came along with its dark sides too. As a matter of fact, social media can really cause a lot of issues for you; it can tamper with your happiness and with your relationships with friends, family, spouse, and co-workers, career, and even health. So what is the way forward? The answer to that question is left to our discretion. Social media is neither good nor bad;

it is what you make it out to be. Last time I checked nobody is physically forced to get on social media, and how you use it is totally up to you. Below are a few examples of how social media can affect us and how we can tone down some of its negative effects and live happier healthier lives even while using it.

Annoying friends/followers

Social media is a platform for the good, the bad, and the others. And the advent of this tool has exposed in many people the excessive need for admiration. To put it politely, Narcissism. Before now we never really had the urge to take pictures of our meals, hairdo, nails, new car, new shop, new boyfriend, etc. But with social media some people feel the excessive need to post pictures so much so it becomes annoying and irritating. Visited the gym? Oh, let's put it out there! Just graduated from college? Let's make a little video and put it on Instagram. Just made a few dollars? Damn right let's take photos of those $5 bills and put it on Facebook. People tend to create a false image of their lives, and it gets old, very old.

What happens is that you begin to abhor such people. And going online only to see annoying people can make using social media a tall order. This can cause a breakdown in your relationship with these persons, and even possibly a breakup.

The way out is to discern why these person(s) need to be endorsed or recognized, then choose whether you want to endorse them or not. Actually when people always seek external approval for almost everything they do it is a clear indication of a low sense of self-worth. They are driven by the fear that they are not good enough, and so they try to do so much to impress their 'friends' on social media. If you know them offline, you could speak to them in person and help build their self-confidence. If not give them the validation they desire, if it doesn't disrupt your own activities, that is, or ignore them totally.

Friendship is a choice

You will always get requests from persons you don't want to be friends with on social media. This happens to all of us. This makes it hard to hide from the prying eyes of some people you'd rather not want to know of your activities online. E.g, co-workers, ex-spouses, former school mates, creditors etc.

If these people are known by you offline it can raise issues if you refuse their online friends request or recognize them as followers. If they sent you a request then that's an indication that they want to be a part of your world, and a 'no' might hurt their feelings.

The way out is to carefully evaluate if you really want them in your life and if they are of any importance to you, and if they are, why not allow them to be your friend or follower on social media. You actually have a lot to lose by ignoring them online. Well, except you don't value their friendship in real life. In the case of an ex, or a stalker you might as well reject their request to save yourself the headache.

Avoid negative people

As I have stated earlier social media has a way of bringing out some of our dark sides. There are folks who are pretty nice when you meet them in person but totally the opposite online. They become mean and insensitive; spreading hate, posting graphic photos, leaving disrespectful comments under people's posts, etc.

The thing is these negative friends on social media can dampen your mood and totally spoil your morning, or evening, or your entire day if not properly handled. They do not do any thinking before they put up a post or upload a picture. Somehow they don't think what they do have any effect on people and think they are safe behind their computer screens.

The way out is to first caution them if you know them offline; talk to them about the potential negative consequence their posts could have, and if they do not listen or you do not know them offline then quickly get rid of them as a friend and/or block them. They may get upset with you for doing that but that's of little consequence; your happiness and mental health are of paramount importance; you need to guard them jealously otherwise some dude behind a computer somewhere will make life miserable for you.

Misconstrued

It's one thing to writing and another to speak. Speaking conveys way more information than writing. When you speak your inflections (intonations), body language, and gesticulations tell most the story much more than writing can. Writing is completely stripped of these body or vocal cues, and people are a lot impatient these days and will not take out the time to really understand what the writer is implying in a post or comment. Also the use of slang and acronyms that are not widely known can also contribute to the problem.

A lot of diatribe and name calling and shaming on social media have stemmed from a simple comment that meant something else (maybe a joke) and was taken to mean another. Plus a lot of users are twitchy about certain topics and wouldn't bear so much as a little opposition, even if it's jocular.

The way out is to be very crystal with your writing. Use smileys and other emojis where necessary to help you better convey your message. Help your readers understand your point of view without using strong or cutting words. Better still don't comment at all if you think it would be taken wrongly. You won't die neither will there be an earthquake or a geostorm if you do not make a comment. Also, resist the urge to reply insults online. Believe me, that's easier said than done but if you are able to overcome you will be better for it; reprisals don't make you feel any better, if anything they make you feel worse because you'd always think you didn't give your best reply.

Safety first

This should be your watch word. Social media can give a persona false sense of safety making you feel like the world is a utopia and all the bad guys are dead. Do not be deceived; the world is a very unsafe place and social media has given bad people an edge, and they are looking to hurt people. Never assume safety, be very sure you are. Do a double or triple check. Some posts or photos you might think are harmless will be used against you. Many people have been robbed or kidnapped because they posted their location on social media. There are people who may get jealous because you posted a photo that makes you look like you are making more progress than they are, and they'll look for ways to hurt you using anything you post. Many ladies have been gang-raped because they keep posting seductive pictures on social media and rudely turning down advances from guys. With their ego bruised, these guys look to get back their pound of flesh.

The way out is to keep your postings minimal and your profiles tight. Because you can upload photos and write posts don't in any way mean you must. Post only when absolutely necessary. And leave your personal lives out of it; nobody really cares if you're at the beach or in your Jacuzzi or on a trip to neverland. Keep all that to yourself. And if that's all you have to post then consider staying off social media temporarily, for your safety.

You are important... just not to them.

The beauty about social media is that it allows you be in direct contact with the big boys, the stars you see on TV and people you passionately admire but aren't in your life offline.

As terrific as this sound, it can have devastating effect on the sense of self-worth of many individuals. You see it's normal to think that because you send a message to people that they should send one right back... okay maybe not immediately but at least sometime before planet Nibiru crashes into earth and end all life. And when they don't you begin to feel worthless, like you don't matter, and then depression comes knocking. A lot of suicide cases have resulted from people feeling they are less than dirt because some star didn't tweet or follow them back or like their comment.

The way out is to relax and understand that you can't control people's actions. They do what they want to do when and how they want to. If they do not reply or follow you back then it means you aren't important to them, which is okay. You are important to some other people. Let's face it, not everyone on planet earth is important to you; there may be someone out there who'd love to be friends with you but you ignore them because they are just not important to you at the moment. Live your life and appreciate yourself, your happiness is your responsibility.

Conclusion

The painful thing is this: Social media is here to stay and won't be going away. I wish I could say it was but I'd be lying through my teeth. But so also will real human life. Real life will also continue even if all social networks were blown away by some cyber-nuke. So therefore it's important that people use their discretion in the use of social media. Social media is awesome, and has no doubt brought the world together more than anything has ever done however, have it in mind that it is not used by itself but by humans who have motives and agendas. And believe me, not everybody's intention is as good as yours. A lot of people project the negativity in their lives on social media and in the process they infect others, and the virus spreads. The best way to get the most out of any social media platform is to:

1. Apply discretion: "Be ye wise as serpents, and harmless as doves", the Bible says. Be smart enough to know the when and how to use social media. Make posts only when absolutely necessary; avoid commenting if it will lead to conflicts. Do not go online when you are upset or over excited about something, otherwise it'll get worse or you might, in your anger, write something you will later regret. Keep personal information to yourself. Nobody really wants to know the color of your poop, or how lousy your neighbor is. Remember: The internet never forgets!

2. Discipline: plan how much time you need to spend on social media, and also what you want to do per session. It's not so good to go on social media just for the fun of it. As abuse is inevitable where purpose is lacking, it is easy to get addicted to it when you have to cogent reason for being on there. What I am saying is: know what you want to do on social media and when

you're done log out and go have a drink with real friends. The mind-control power of these platforms comes from staying too long on them with any purpose for being there.

3. Prioritize: know what's more important at the moment. And if you ask me, I'd say your offline life is. As good as Social media is it shouldn't replace your actual life. Do not sacrifice your life on the altar of Facebook or instagram, nothing is a worthy substitute for your life offline. Whatever life you build online is completely virtual and can be wiped out with a little tweak in one line of the platforms algorithm code. Keep in mind that you had values before you went on social media; don't trade them for a few "likes".

4. Fast: okay this may not seem like an appropriate title for this point but let me explain. I'd recommend taking some time off social media, maybe a month. This will

be very rewarding I assure you. If you have business online you may not be able to switch off completely, so use it very sparingly during your 'fast' period. Go hiking, surfing, or flying. Basically, whatever it is you love to do offline. And do not take pictures to post on your social media profile; do this for you to get rid of the heaviness that can come from being online too long.

As they say, "A word is enough for the wise". Remember social media is neither good nor bad; it is what you make it to be. Thank you for reading, I hope it was helpful.